Specialty Beads:

Large Glass Beads

Pearl White Seed Beads

Pastel Seed Beads

Primary Seed Beads

Tip: Have your beads conveniently at your finger tips by storing them in small parts boxes, medicine bottles or baby food jars.

ellow-Green eed Beads

Jewel Tone Seed Beads

Bright Color Seed Beads

Blue & Blues Seed Beads

White & Violet Seed Beads

Violet & Pinks Seed Beads

Soft Hue Seed Beads

Clear

Crystal

Gold

Silver

Dark Bugles

Pale Bugles

Best Book of Beading 3

Helpful Tools

Around the House Supplies

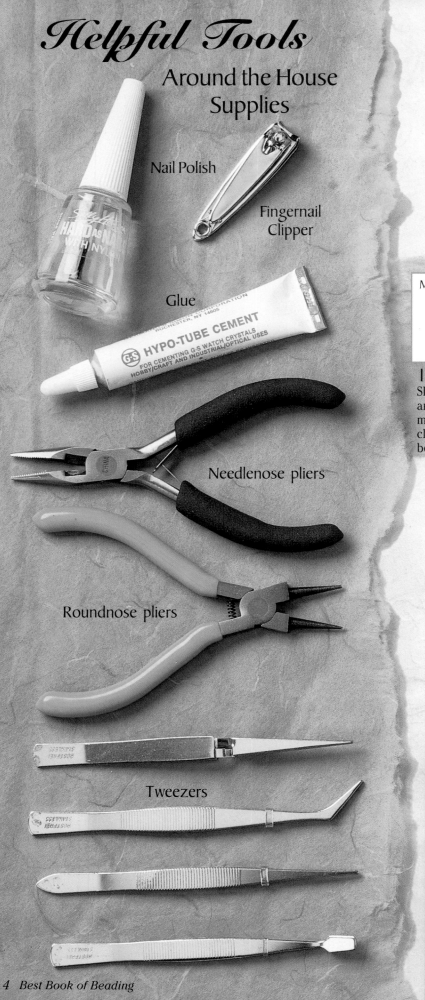

Nail Polish

Fingernail Clipper

Glue

Needlenose pliers

Roundnose pliers

Tweezers

The Basics

Crimp Beads and Monofilament

Monofilament

Crimp Bead

Barrel Clasp

1. **Begin** Necklace or Bracelet: Slide a crimp bead on monofilament. Thread one end of monofilament through loop of clasp, and back through crimp bead, leaving 1/2" tail.

2. Slide crimp bead up close to clasp, leaving a small space between crimp and clasp. Squeeze crimp bead flat with pliers.

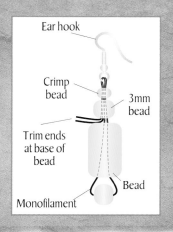

Ear hook

Crimp bead

3mm bead

Trim ends at base of bead

Monofilament

Bead

Loop Earrings

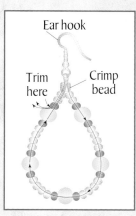

Ear hook

Trim here

Crimp bead

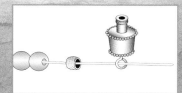

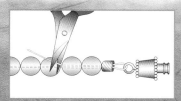

3. Thread a few beads covering part of the monofilament tail. Do not cut off tail until necklace or bracelet is complete.

4. **End** Necklace or Bracelet: After the last bead, slide a crimp bead on monofilament. Thread end of monofilament through the other half of clasp.

5. Thread monofilament back through crimp and beads. Hold clasp, pull tail up taut. Leave a space between crimp and clasp. Squeeze crimp flat with pliers.

6. Cut off monofilament tails with scissors as close as possible to the bead. The end of tails will be hidden between beads.

I Strand Glass Bead Bracelet

Tip: For a braided necklace, use transparent tape to secure braid together while attaching clasp.

3 Strand Twist Necklace

I Strand Necklace

2 Strand Twist Necklace

3 Strand Braid Necklace

Easy Glass Bead Necklace

Japanese Beads

Seed Beads

E-Beads

Bugle Beads

Glass Beads

Tube Bead

Log Bead

Disc Bead

Pearls

3 mm Pearls

5 mm Pearls

Red & Blue Necklace

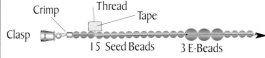

Crimp   Thread   Tape   Clasp

15 Seed Beads   3 E-Beads

1. Begin like Basic Necklace, but do not flatten crimp bead. Leave 6" tail on thread. Hold tail in place with good tape. String 15 seed beads, 3 E-beads; repeat 13 times.

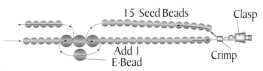

15 Seed Beads   Clasp

Add 1 E-Bead   Crimp

2. End with 15 seed beads, crimp bead, and other end of clasp. Go back through crimp bead, add 15 seed beads. Do not flatten crimp bead.

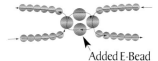

Added E-Bead

3. Follow thread path in diagram #2 to make flower. After pulling snug, necklace will look like diagram #3.

End   Trim End

Clasp   Trim End

Crimp   Begin

4. At end of necklace, go through crimp bead, clasp and crimp bead. Take thread back through a few seed beads. Snug up beads, flatten crimp beads on both ends. Trim tails of thread.

Easy Jewelry

Needle & Thread

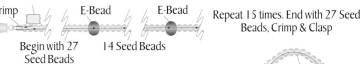

Choker Necklace - Repeat the beading pattern until you have reached the desired length.

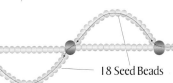

Crimp   E-Bead   E-Bead   Repeat 15 times. End with 27 Seed Beads, Crimp & Clasp

Begin with 27 Seed Beads   14 Seed Beads

Figure '8' Necklace - Begin as in Basic Necklace, but do not flatten crimp bead. Leave 6" tail. Add beads as shown. At  18 Seed Beads
the end, add a crimp bead and clasp; go back through the ending 27 seed beads and the first E bead. Add 18 seed beads, go through the next E bead; repeat to the end of necklace, passing thread back through the first 27 seed beads. Pull snug; crimp beads. Trim tails.

Beaded Daisy Chain - Repeat the pattern until you have reached the desired length.

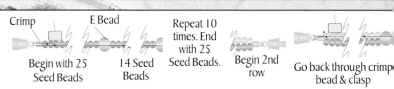

Crimp   E Bead   Repeat 10 times. End with 25 Seed Beads.   Begin 2nd row   Go back through crimp bead & clasp

Begin with 25 Seed Beads   14 Seed Beads

Multi Strand Necklace - Begin and end as in Basic Necklace, but do not flatten crimp beads. Leave 6" tail. Add beads as shown. Repeat for each color of seed bead, going through the same E bead with each strand. Snug up thread; flatten crimp beads. Trim ends. Begin 3rd row

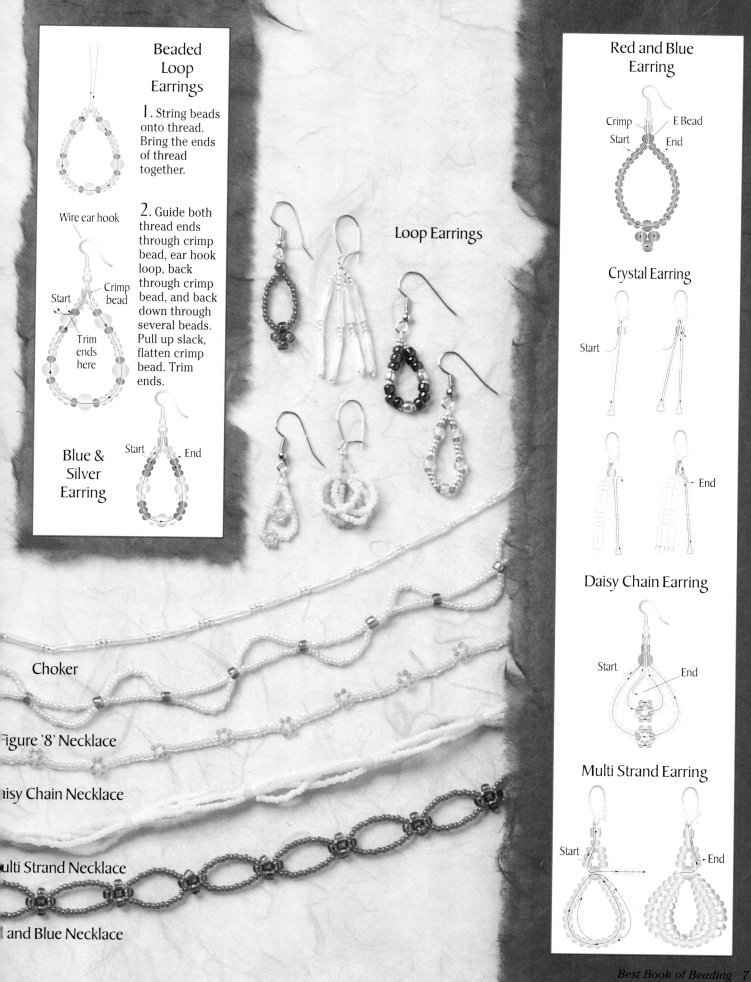

Beaded Loop Earrings

1. String beads onto thread. Bring the ends of thread together.

2. Guide both thread ends through crimp bead, ear hook loop, back through crimp bead, and back down through several beads. Pull up slack, flatten crimp bead. Trim ends.

Wire ear hook

Crimp bead

Start

Trim ends here

Blue & Silver Earring

Start   End

Loop Earrings

Red and Blue Earring

Crimp   E Bead

Start   End

Crystal Earring

Start

End

Daisy Chain Earring

Start   End

Multi Strand Earring

Start   End

Choker

Figure '8' Necklace

aisy Chain Necklace

ulti Strand Necklace

and Blue Necklace

Dangles

Head Pins & Eye Pins

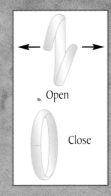

Tip: Open and close your jumprings side to side using needle nose pliers as shown.

1. Thread beads on a head or eye pin. Clip end of pin to $3/8$" and bend at a 90 degree angle.

2. Curve end into a loop with round nose pliers.

3. Slip end loop on ear wire, hook or jumpring.

4. Make a single head p[in] dangle or connect eye p[ins] dangles together and atta[ch] an ear hook.

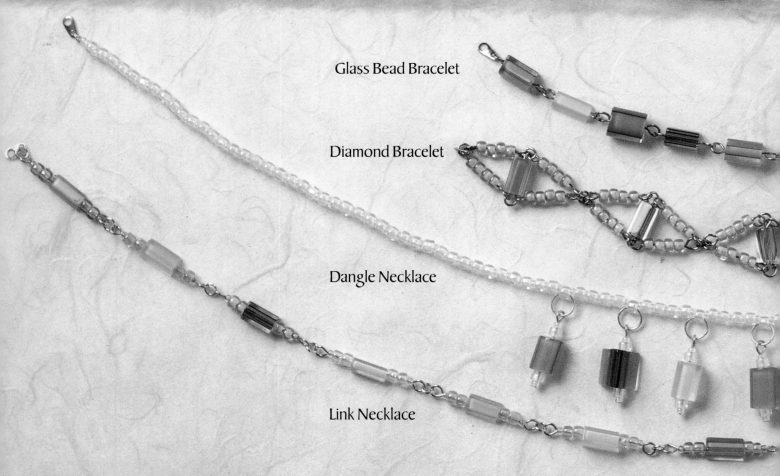

Glass Bead Bracelet

Diamond Bracelet

Dangle Necklace

Link Necklace

Dangle Earrings

5. Use a head pin to make a single dangle or combine a head pin and eye pin to make a double link earring.

6. Let the long shaft of the eye pin become part of the earring design or shorten it to change the look completely.

Glass Bead Bracelet

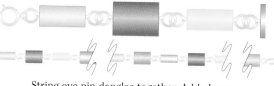

String eye pin dangles together. Add clasp.

Diamond Bracelet

String eye pin dangles together; add jumprings and clasp.

Dangle Necklace

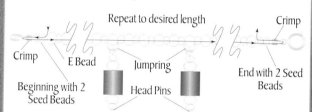

Crimp · Repeat to desired length · Crimp

E Bead · Jumpring

Beginning with 2 Seed Beads · Head Pins · End with 2 Seed Beads

String seed beads and E beads to desired necklace length. Attach head pin dangles to E beads with jumprings.

Link Necklace

Make dangles using eye pins. Link dangles together using jumprings. Attach clasp.

Birthday Stones

Make any piece of jewelry special. Choose favorite colors or birthday stones.

Birthstones

January	Garnet	July	Ruby
February	Amethyst	August	Peridot
March	Aquamarine	September	Sapphire
April	Diamond	October	Opal
May	Emerald	November	Topaz
June	Alexandrite	December	Zircon

Hair Accessories

Combs, Pins, Clips & Hair Bands

Beading Wire

Snap-On Barrette

Bobby Pin

Bobby Pin with Pad

Bobby Pin

Curved Clip-On

Clip-On Rectangle

Snap-On Hair Clip

Hair Comb

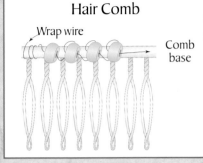

Wrap wire

Comb base

Wrap wire around comb base, pull tight. Add bead, wrap, pull tight and repeat to end of base. Wrap wire.

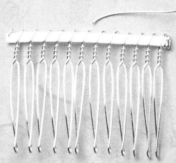

Comb

Hair Band

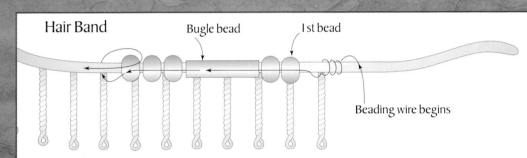

Bugle bead

1st bead

Beading wire begins

Wrap wire around hair band base behind first hair prong. Begin beading: 2 E-beads, bugle bead, 3 E-beads. Wrap wire around hair band base at third E-bead. Continue: Add bugle bead and 3 E-beads. Wrap wire around base at third E-bead. Repeat. End beading with 2 E-beads, wrap wire same as at beginning.

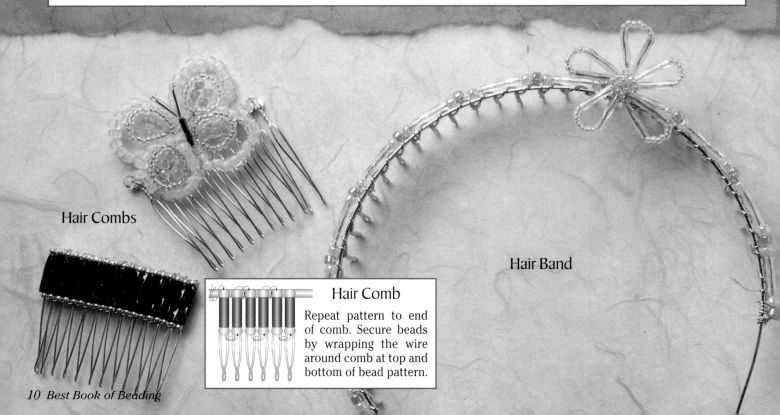

Hair Combs

Hair Band

Hair Comb

Repeat pattern to end of comb. Secure beads by wrapping the wire around comb at top and bottom of bead pattern.

Hair Pins & Clips

Thread 30 beads for each wing; make 4. Add 3 bugle beads to end of one wire for tail; curl end to secure. Add large bead to new wire for body; curl end to secure. Wire body to wings; wire to pin.

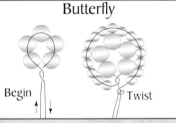

Dragonfly

Daisy Flower

a   b   c   d

String 17 beads for petal. Twist. Make 9 petals. String 21 beads for stem. Curl wire. String flower center.

Flower Center

Wrap wire around center of petals

Heart

Start Here

Use one wire.

Butterfly

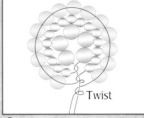

Begin   Twist   Twist

1. For butterfly wings, thread Violet beads on wire. Twist wire to secure beads. Thread Silver beads. Twist wire to secure beads.

2. Thread Pink beads on wire. Twist wire. Wing is complete. Make four wings and twist all wires together. Wrap wires around hair pin.

3. To make the butterfly body, curl 2 wires using round nose pliers. Thread through Silver bugle beads and a large yellow glass bead. Twist wire.

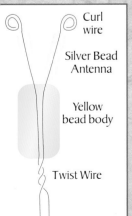

Curl wire

Silver Bead Antenna

Yellow bead body

Twist Wire

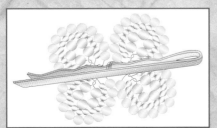

4. Wrap body around wings. Wrap butterfly around pin with wire.

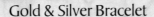

Gold & Silver Bracelet

Pastel Flower Bracelet

Wide Bugle Bead Bracelet

Beading Loom

Bracelets & Necklaces

Wide Bugle Bead Bracelet

Beading Pattern

Repeat pattern

Loom Beading Pattern
Left side of loom

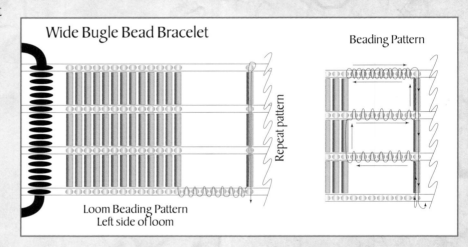

Beaded Ball Closure

1. Use large bead the same color as seed beads. Follow diagram to begin.

2. Continue wrapping small beads around large bead, knotting and pulling tight until large bead is covered.

Covered ball

3. Add more beads to both strands of thread.

Knot on warp thread

Loomed Bracelet

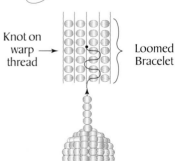

4. Weave thread ends back and forth through beads and tie off with knot on warp thread.

Amulet Bag

Tip: Use warp threads for loops and to attach ball or bead.

· For pendants, warp loom with extra long thread. Use for fringe.

· Always wrap a long warp. Beading thread is cheap and it is always better to have too much rather than too little!

· Make ball end of closure first. When making loop, be sure it is long enough to go around ball closure.

Dragonfly Necklace

Butterfly Necklace

Gold and Silver Bracelet

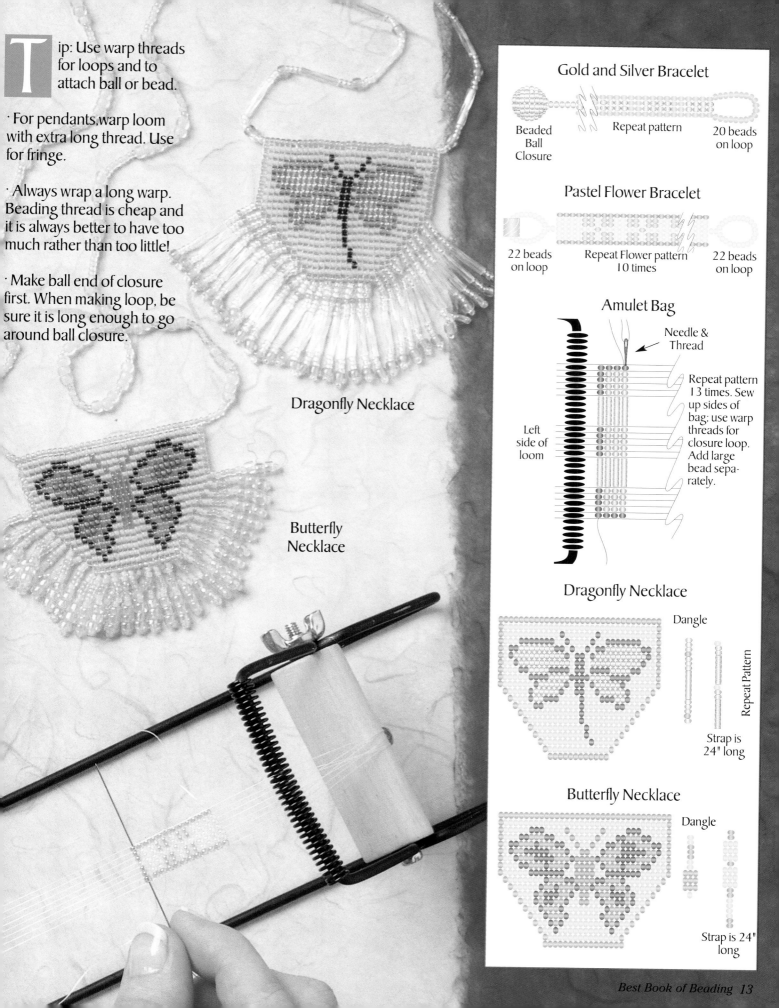

Beaded Ball Closure

Repeat pattern

20 beads on loop

Pastel Flower Bracelet

22 beads on loop

Repeat Flower pattern 10 times

22 beads on loop

Amulet Bag

Needle & Thread

Left side of loom

Repeat pattern 13 times. Sew up sides of bag; use warp threads for closure loop. Add large bead separately.

Dragonfly Necklace

Dangle

Repeat Pattern

Strap is 24" long

Butterfly Necklace

Dangle

Strap is 24" long

Beaded Purses

Glitz & Glitter for Evening

Beaded Purse Netting

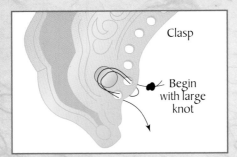

Clasp

Begin with large knot

1. Tie a knot around two hole spaces, with knot to the inside. Follow diagram to put one E-bead at side of clasp.

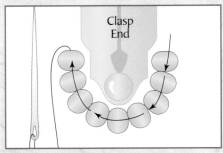

Clasp End

2. On small purse, thread six Gold E-beads with a Gold seed bead in between each one.
On large purse, thread 10 Silver E-beads.

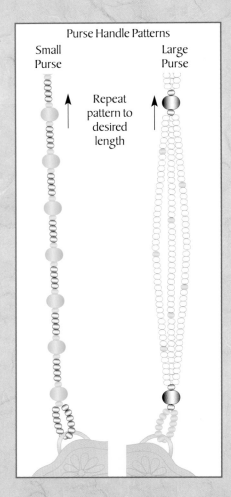

Purse Handle Patterns

Small Purse

Large Purse

Repeat pattern to desired length

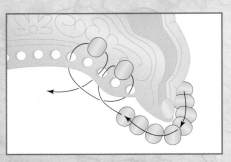

3. Continue covering the holes on the purse frame.
On small frame, use one Gold E-bead for every two holes.
On large purse, use one Silver E-bead per hole.

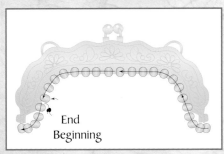

End Beginning

4. On small purse run thread back up to and out the 5th bead from the end.
Small purse netting pattern: 1 Gold, 3 Silver lined, 1 Gold seed, 1 Gold E-bead, repeat. On large purse go back up to and out of the 6th bead from the end.
Large purse netting pattern: 1 Silver, 1 Gold, 3 Clear, 1 Gold, 1 Silver seed, 1 Silver E-bead; repeat seed beads.

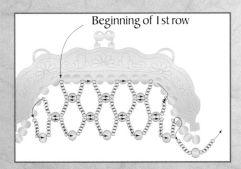

Beginning of 1st row

5. Work the first 3 rows on one side of frame; continue around purse by adding another netting loop under the side loop. Return thread for beginning of 1st row. At end of the 3rd row, add another loop under the side loop to complete 3rd row.

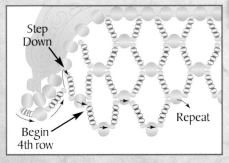

Step Down

Begin 4th row

Repeat

6. You must "step down" to begin the 4th row, and between succeeding rows. See thread path diagram.
You may wish to put fewer beads in the netting loop on the last 3 or 4 rows to tighten the netting for the purse bottom. Weave together at purse bottom; knot.

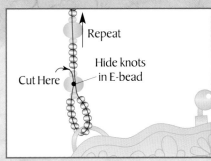

Repeat

Hide knots in E-bead

Cut Here

7. Use at least 2 threads in handles for added strength. Hide knots in E-bead.

3-D Flowers

Beaded Broaches & More

1. Thread beads on wire and twist. Add center bead. Thread more beads on 2nd loop. Twist. Return wire through center bead.

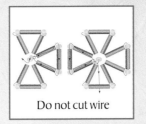

Do not cut wire

2. Continue adding beads until four or five loops are made. Twist. Let wire hang free; do not cut wire.

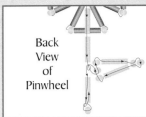

Back View of Pinwheel

3. Add beads as shown in di gram for stem and leaf. Twi wire. Thread end wire back through bugle bead.

Pinwheel Flower

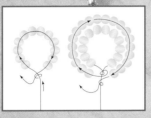

1. Pansy Petals: Thread beads on wire for 1st and 2nd rows, twisting wire after each row.

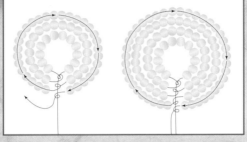

2. Add beads for 3rd and 4th rows, twisting wire after each row to secure beads.

3. Twist off last row of beads and loop wire over 3 rows of beads toward center. Add 4 beads to wire.

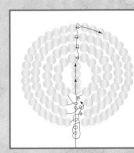

4. Loop bead wire ov top 4 rows and threa wire back through bead to finish petal/leaf.

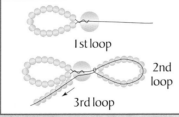

1st loop

2nd loop

3rd loop

1. Easy Loop Flower: Thread beads on wire and twist. Add large bead. Thread more beads for second loop. Twist. Return wire through large bead.

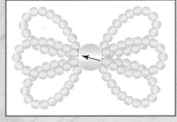

2. Repeat Step 1 until six loops are made. Twist. Thread wire back through large bead.

3. Fan petals out to form flower. Make one pink and one white.

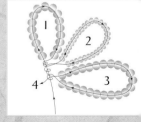

1

2

3

4

1. Twist Flower: Threa beads on wire and twis Add more beads and twi wire around 1st twist. Co tinue until flower is as fr as desired. Wire flowe around pin back.

Twist Flower Ribbon Necklace

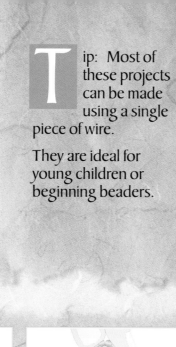

Tip: Most of these projects can be made using a single piece of wire.

They are ideal for young children or beginning beaders.

Easy Loop Flower Brooch

Red Berry Ball

Thread beads on large ball until covered. Add beads for stem.

Red Berries Pin

Pansy Pin

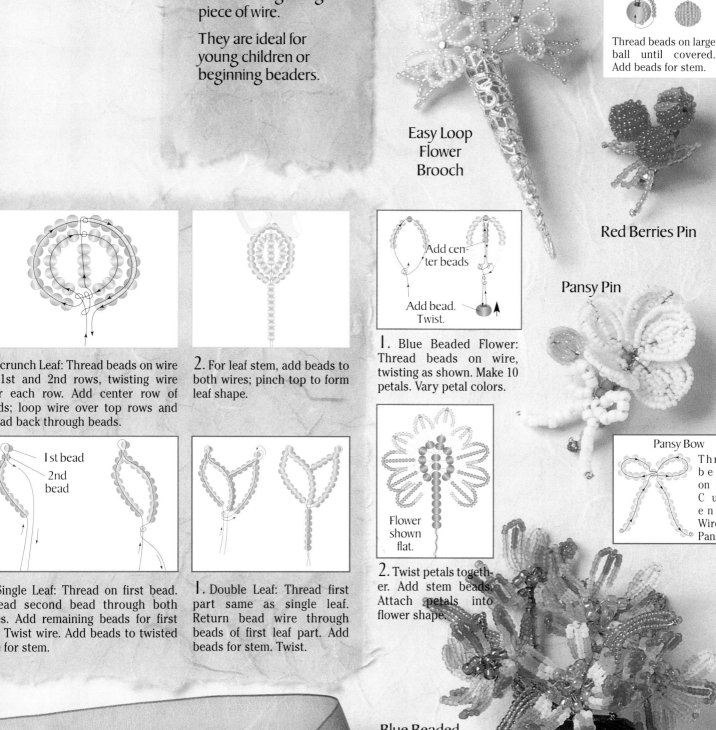

. Scrunch Leaf: Thread beads on wire r 1st and 2nd rows, twisting wire ter each row. Add center row of ads; loop wire over top rows and read back through beads.

2. For leaf stem, add beads to both wires; pinch top to form leaf shape.

1. Blue Beaded Flower: Thread beads on wire, twisting as shown. Make 10 petals. Vary petal colors.

Add center beads

Add bead. Twist.

1st bead

2nd bead

. Single Leaf: Thread on first bead. read second bead through both res. Add remaining beads for first af. Twist wire. Add beads to twisted re for stem.

1. Double Leaf: Thread first part same as single leaf. Return bead wire through beads of first leaf part. Add beads for stem. Twist.

Flower shown flat.

2. Twist petals together. Add stem beads. Attach petals into flower shape.

Pansy Bow

Thread beads on wire. Curl ends. Wire to Pansies.

Blue Beaded Arrangement

Bottle Draping

Beautiful Beaded Display Pieces

Sun Catcher

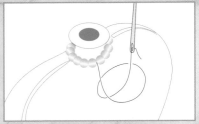

1. Knot thread. Add first row of beads around bottle neck. Knot thread to end 1st row.

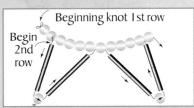

2. Add 2 bugle beads, 1 E-bead, 2 bugle beads. Thread through 1st row of E-beads.

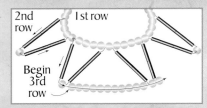

3. To begin 3rd row, drop down through 2 bugle beads and E-bead. Begin adding E beads.

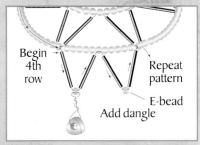

4. To begin 4th row, add 2 bugle beads, E-bead, 2 bugle beads, up through 3rd row E-bead and repeat. Make dangles using eye pin and nugget bead.

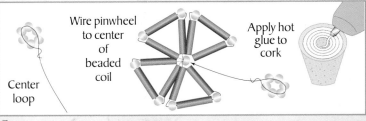

5. Beaded Cork Bottle Top: Thread beads on wire for center loop of beaded coil. Twist. Make pinwheel following directions on page 16; steps 1 & 2. Wire pinwheel to center of beaded coil. Add beads to bottom wire as needed to cover cork top. Squeeze hot glue on top of cork. Press center of beaded coil with pinwheel onto cork center. Continue pressing and winding beads onto top of cork until cork is covered.